GRAPHIC MODERN HISTORY: WORLD WAR I

WAR AT SEA

By Gary Jeffrey & Illustrated by Terry Riley

Crabtree Publishing Company
www.crabtreebooks.com

Crabtree Publishing Company

www.crabtreebooks.com

Created and produced by:
    David West Children's Books

Project development, design, and concept:
    David West Children's Books

Author and designer: Gary Jeffrey

Illustrator: Terry Riley

Editor: Lynn Peppas

Proofreader: Kelly McNiven

Project coordinator: Kathy Middleton

Print and production coordinator:
    Katherine Berti

Prepress technician: Katherine Berti

Photographs: p5r, Bundesarchiv

Library and Archives Canada Cataloguing in Publication

Jeffrey, Gary
        War at sea / Gary Jeffrey ; illustrated by Terry Riley.

(Graphic modern history : World War I)
Includes index.
Issued also in electronic formats.
ISBN 978-0-7787-0913-8 (bound).
--ISBN 978-0-7787-0923-7 (pbk.)

        1. World War, 1914-1918--Naval operations--Juvenile
literature. 2. World War, 1914-1918--Naval operations--Comic
books, strips, etc. 3. Graphic novels. I. Riley, Terry II. Title.
III. Series: Jeffrey, Gary. Graphic modern history. World War I.

D580.J35 2013   j940.4'5   C2013-901125-0

Library of Congress Cataloging-in-Publication Data

Jeffrey, Gary.
  War at sea / Gary Jeffrey ; illustrated by Terry Riley.
        pages cm. -- (Graphic modern history : World War I)
  Includes index.
  Audience: Ages 10-13.
  ISBN 978-0-7787-0913-8 (reinforced library binding) -- ISBN
978-0-7787-0923-7 (pbk.) -- ISBN 978-1-4271-9256-1 (electronic
pdf) -- ISBN 978-1-4271-9180-9 (electronic html)
  1. World War, 1914-1918--Naval operations--Pictorial works--
Juvenile literature. I. Riley, Terry, illustrator. II. Title. III. Title:
World War I.

  D581.J34 2013
  940.4'5--dc23

                                            2013005532

Crabtree Publishing Company

www.crabtreebooks.com   1-800-387-7650

Printed in the U.S.A./042013/SX20130306

Published in Canada
Crabtree Publishing
616 Welland Ave.
St. Catharines, Ontario
L2M 5V6

Published in the United States
Crabtree Publishing
PMB 59051
350 Fifth Avenue, 59th Floor
New York, New York 10118

Published in the United Kingdom
Crabtree Publishing
Maritime House
Basin Road North, Hove
BN41 1WR

Published in Australia
Crabtree Publishing
3 Charles Street
Coburg North
VIC 3058

CONTENTS

SEA POWER

In 1899, when Imperial Germany began building up its navy, an arms race began with Great Britain that would ultimately be decided by the clash of steel dreadnoughts on the high seas.

Britain's HMS Dreadnought *(1906) was the first all-big-gun battleship and gave her name to all the big battleships of WWI.*

U-boats lie docked at Kiel in north Germany. On the far right, in the first row, is U-21, which fired the first ever self-propelled torpedo in combat to score a kill.

UNDERSEA ATTACKS

When war broke out, Germany's navy, although powerfully equipped, was still outnumbered by Britain's Grand Fleet. A small submarine fleet of U-boats was dispatched instead. Their task was to clear the sea lanes that were being blocked by British patrols.

On September 5, 1914, U-21 sighted the Royal Navy Scout Cruiser HMS *Pathfinder*. Her single torpedo hit the ship's boiler, exploding the magazine.

WARSHIPS CLASH

The British, meanwhile, took the battle to the Germans by raiding ships close to the German coast, at Heligoland Bight. On August 28, 1914, two flotillas of more than 30 destroyers hit German torpedo

boats but found themselves outgunned by cruisers. A backup squadron of Royal Navy battleships came to the rescue, and sank three of the light cruisers. Britain had gained a crucial first victory in the war between ships.

SMS Mainz *sank with a Rear Admiral onboard at Heligoland.*

The German East Asia Squadron, commanded by Vice Admiral Maximilian von Spee (inset) on *Scharnhorst*, was isolated, and doomed to fight until its ammunition ran out.

SQUADRON OF DOOM

The losses at Heligoland made the German Kaiser, or Emperor, reluctant to risk his home fleet in open battle. Meanwhile, the German's East Asia Squadron scored a great victory when it sank two British cruisers off the coast of central Chile on November 1, 1914. A task force, headed by two battlecruisers, was dispatched, and engaged Von Spee's raiders at the Falkland Islands. Four of the five were sunk, including *Scharnhorst*.

Bombardment of the British coast by German ships on December 16, 1914, caused outrage.

The liner RMS Lusitania was sunk by a U-boat on May, 7, 1915, with the loss of 1,195 civilians.

INFAMY

In 1915, the waters around Britain had been declared a war zone by the Germans, who were determined to sink as many merchant ships as possible. The British, in their turn, tightened their blockade, hoping to starve Germany out. The two navies had to come to grips and battle it out.

The British intercepted German radio traffic, resulting in armored cruiser Blücher being hounded and sunk off Dogger bank on Britain's east coast on January 24, 1915.

SHOWDOWN AT JUTLAND

In 1916, the Kaiserliche Marine received a new commander, Vice Admiral Scheer, who persuaded the Kaiser to use the High Seas Fleet more aggressively against the British.

Scheer planned to level the odds for the German Navy.

RENDEZVOUS AT SKAGERRAK

On April 25, 1916, unrestricted submarine war was halted by the Germans. This was partly to appease the United States, which had been protesting over the sinking of its merchant vessels. More importantly, it freed the U-boats so they could be grouped to lie in wait outside the harbors that held Admiral Jellicoe's Grand Fleet. The German ships would then be sent to attack the British coast, to lure their fleet out into the submarine trap.

But the British had broken the Imperial naval code and, as soon as Scheer left port, sent a force of their own to intercept him. Bad weather hampered the U-boat action. The two fleets met at Skagerrak off Jutland, Denmark.

Admiral Jellicoe was cautious, and aware that he could lose the war "in an afternoon" if a major battle took place.

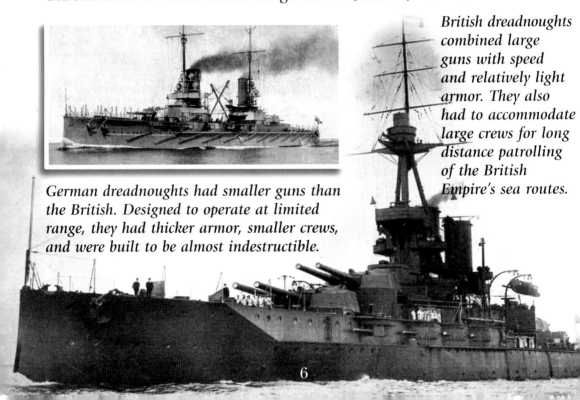

German dreadnoughts had smaller guns than the British. Designed to operate at limited range, they had thicker armor, smaller crews, and were built to be almost indestructible.

British dreadnoughts combined large guns with speed and relatively light armor. They also had to accommodate large crews for long distance patrolling of the British Empire's sea routes.

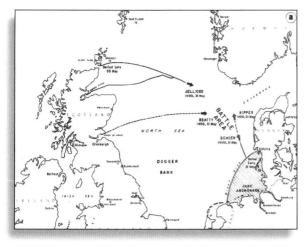

The British ships left from three bases and steamed east to meet two groups of German ships.

Opening Acts

Ahead of both the German and British dreadnoughts steamed scouting squadrons of battlecruisers. These had the same guns as the battleships but were faster, with lighter armor. The opposing battlecruisers came within range of each other in the late afternoon. The German commander, Hipper, attempted to lure the British battlecruisers into a trap (see page 18).

The Fleets Engage

The British battlecruiser commander, Beatty, headed north to draw Scheer's entire force towards Jellicoe.

Three hours later, the British forces finally met up, but could not locate the Germans. Jellicoe, in one of the most momentous decisions of the war, decided to head east. Meanwhile, Hipper's battlecruisers took a massive pummeling, but destroyed HMS *Invincible* in return.

Scheer was suddenly taken by surprise as his column of ships met the fire arc of the entire 28 British dreadnought line. Scheer ordered his fleet to turn and run, and, although the battle continued, he was able to break out his damaged ships, and escape back to Germany in the night.

Fast battleships HMS **Warspite** *and* **Malaya** *steam into action at Jutland.*

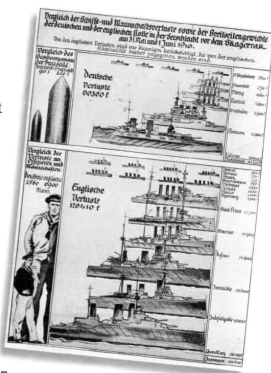

A German poster announces their losses versus British losses—three British battlecruisers for one German battlecruiser, among other ships.

SECOND BLOOD TO U-9

SEPTEMBER 22, 1914, IN THE NORTH SEA OFF THE COAST OF HOLLAND.

AT 06:15 HRS, U-9 OF THE GERMAN IMPERIAL NAVY SLIPPED SMOOTHLY BENEATH THE WAVES.

HER COMMANDER, KAPITANLEUTNANT OTTO WEDDIGEN, TOOK A LAST LOOK THROUGH THE PERISCOPE.

EXCELLENT, WE'RE ALMOST THERE.

HE WAS POSITIONED CAREFULLY. BAD WEATHER HAD SO FAR FRUSTRATED HIS EFFORTS TO ENGAGE BRITISH WARSHIPS BLOCKING THE GERMAN SEA ROUTES.

BUT TODAY THE WEATHER WAS CLEAR AND CALM.

FULL STOP!

THE THREE ARMORED CRUISERS HAD NO IDEA WHAT WAS COMING.

FIRE ONE.

A TORPEDO SHOT FROM THE STARBOARD TUBE.

PHOOSH

THE SHIPS WERE HMS CRESSY, ABOUKIR, AND HOGUE. THE STORMS HAD ALSO CHASED AWAY THEIR DESTROYER ESCORTS. MANNED BY PART-TIME RESERVISTS AND CADETS, THEY WERE SITTING DUCKS.

THE TORPEDO STRUCK ABOUKIR'S BEAM.

KROOM!

THE EXPLOSION BLEW OPEN THE HULL, FLOODING THE ENGINE ROOM.

WE CAN ONLY GET ONE BOAT AWAY. THE STEAM-POWERED WINCHES WON'T WORK.

UNLEASH THE DECK TIMBERS. GET ANYTHING INTO THE WATER THAT'LL FLOAT!

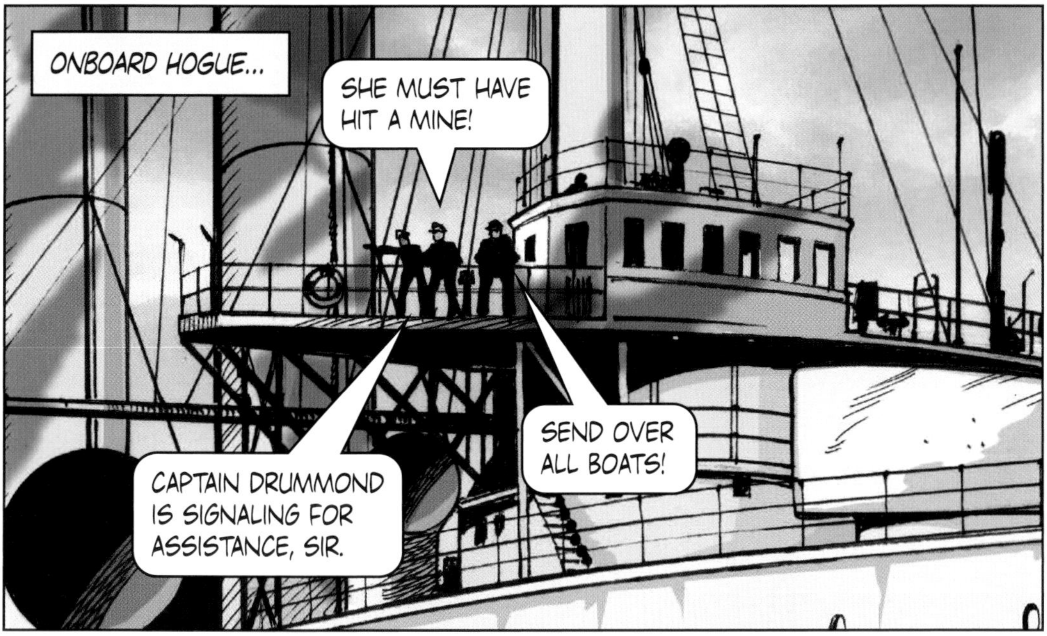
ONBOARD HOGUE...
SHE MUST HAVE HIT A MINE!
CAPTAIN DRUMMOND IS SIGNALING FOR ASSISTANCE, SIR.
SEND OVER ALL BOATS!

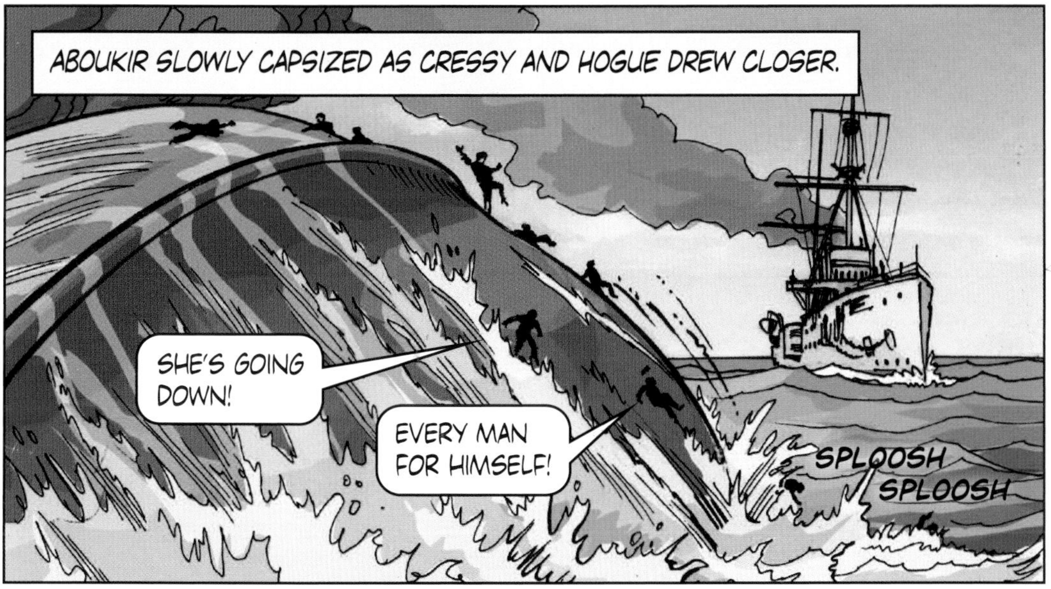
ABOUKIR SLOWLY CAPSIZED AS CRESSY AND HOGUE DREW CLOSER.
SHE'S GOING DOWN!
EVERY MAN FOR HIMSELF!
SPLOOSH
SPLOOSH

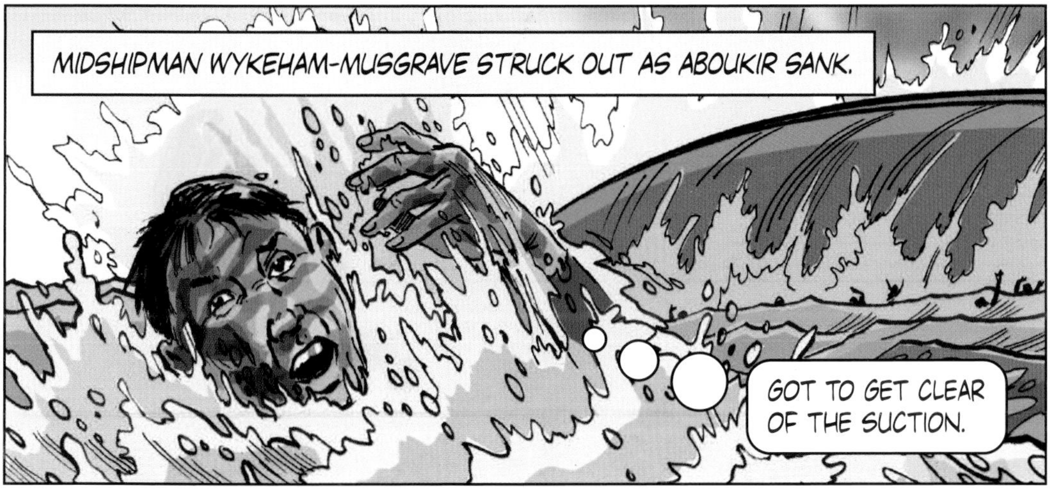
MIDSHIPMAN WYKEHAM-MUSGRAVE STRUCK OUT AS ABOUKIR SANK.
GOT TO GET CLEAR OF THE SUCTION.

WEDDIGEN WATCHED AS HOGUE CAME IN RANGE.

THEY HAVEN'T SEEN US...

...WE DON'T EVEN NEED TO CHANGE POSITION.

FIRE TWO!

FLOOSH!

FLOOSH!

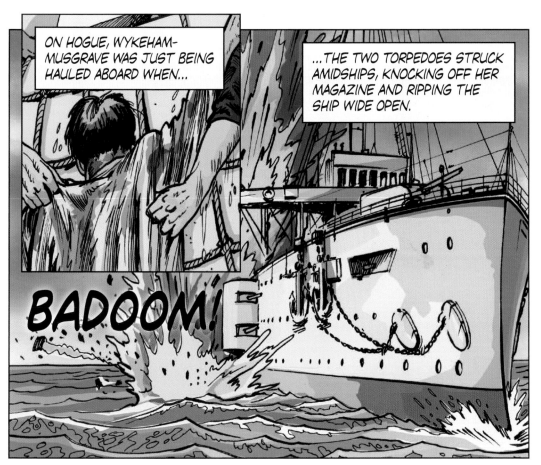

ON HOGUE, WYKEHAM-MUSGRAVE WAS JUST BEING HAULED ABOARD WHEN...

...THE TWO TORPEDOES STRUCK AMIDSHIPS, KNOCKING OFF HER MAGAZINE AND RIPPING THE SHIP WIDE OPEN.

BADOOM!

ONBOARD CRESSY...

PERISCOPE OFF THE PORT BOW!

STRAIGHT FOR HER! RAMMING SPEED!

BOON!

PLOOSH!

BUT U-9 SLIPPED UNDER THE WAVES, AVOIDING CRESSY'S BOW.

THRUM!
THRUM!
THRUM!

GREEEEEEEEE

A FEW MOMENTS LATER, WEDDIGEN SURFACED AGAIN.

THEY'VE LAID OFF THE ATTACK, AND MANEUVERED AROUND THE SECOND SHIP TO PICK UP SURVIVORS.

HE MANEUVERED THE U-9 TO BE FACING **AWAY** FROM CRESSY.

FIVE DEGREES MORE...

GREEEEEEE

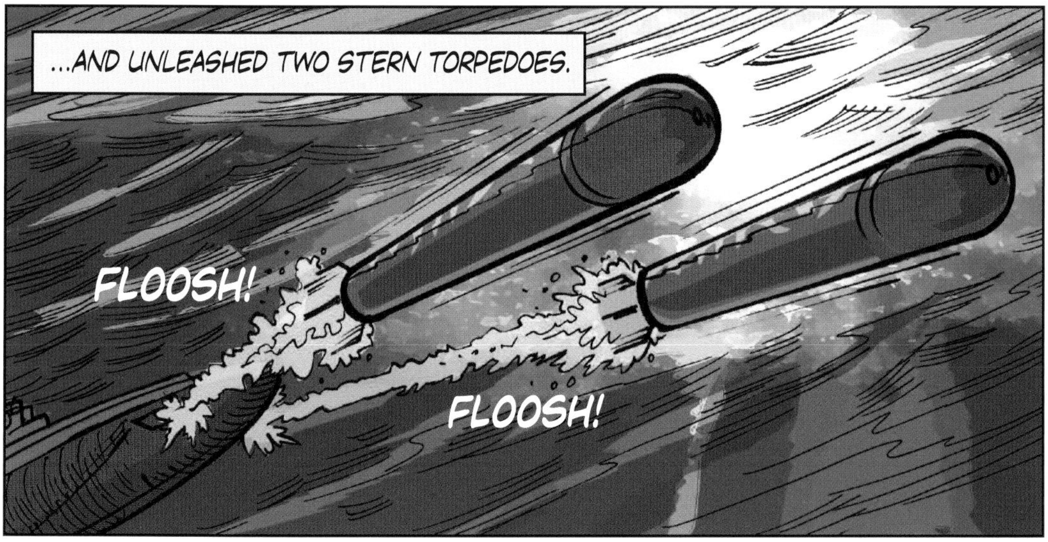
...AND UNLEASHED TWO STERN TORPEDOES.
FLOOSH!
FLOOSH!

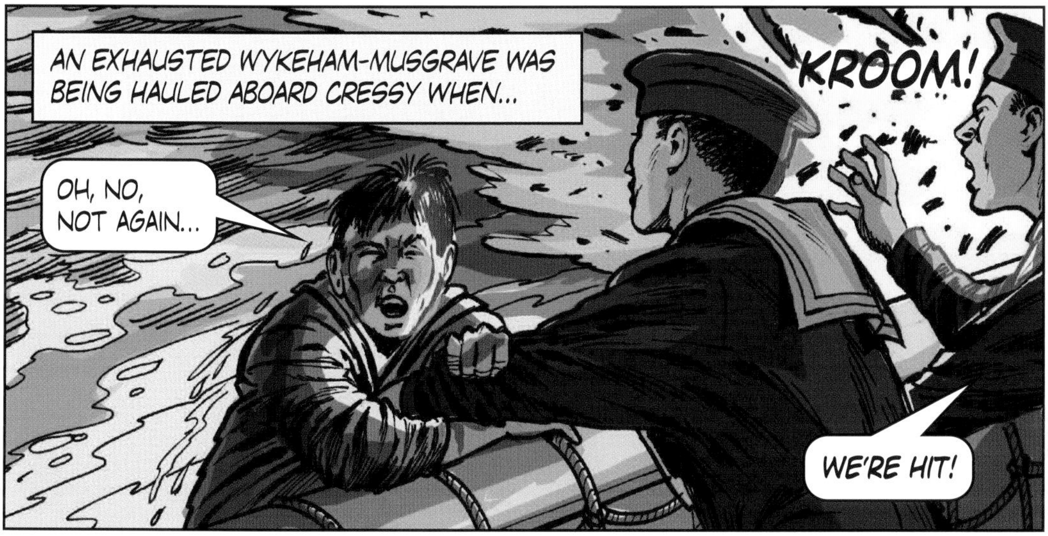
AN EXHAUSTED WYKEHAM-MUSGRAVE WAS BEING HAULED ABOARD CRESSY WHEN...
KROOM!
OH, NO, NOT AGAIN...
WE'RE HIT!

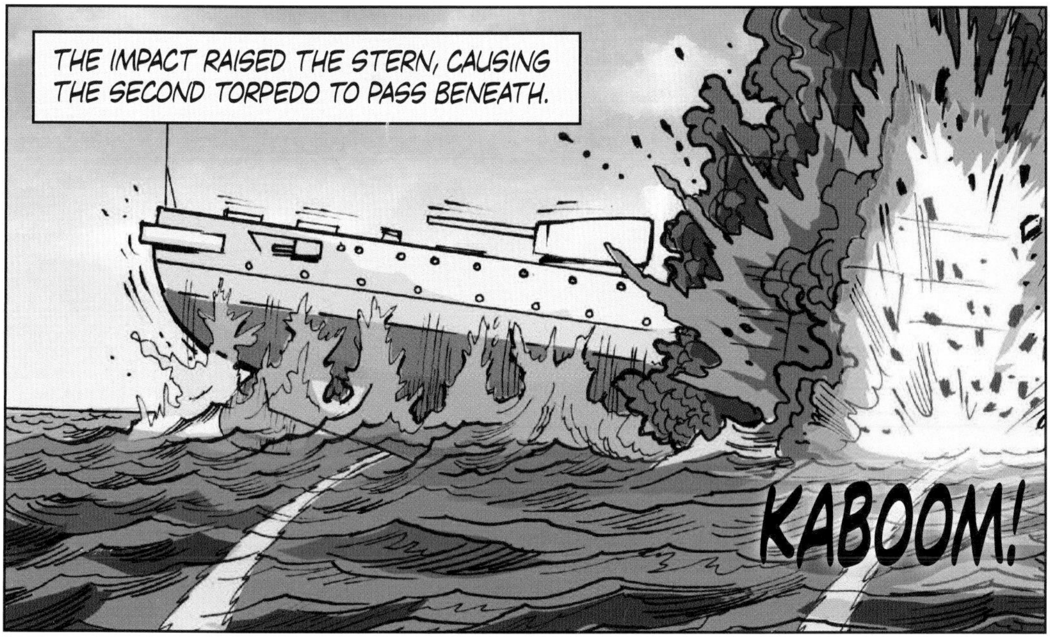
THE IMPACT RAISED THE STERN, CAUSING THE SECOND TORPEDO TO PASS BENEATH.
KABOOM!

BRING US ABOUT.

WEDDIGEN HAD ONE TORPEDO LEFT.

WITHIN MINUTES, IT WAS HEADING STRAIGHT TOWARD THE MIDDLE OF THE CRESSY.

SCHWEEEE

AS BOILER ROOM FIVE ERUPTED IN FLAMES, THE MEN THREW THEMSELVES INTO THE WATER.

BOOM

WYKEHAM-MUSGRAVE LASHED HIMSELF TO A PIECE OF TIMBER, AND PASSED OUT.

URRRGH...

HER BATTERY POWER NEARLY EXHAUSTED, U-9 SPED AWAY FROM THE SCENE. WEIGHED DOWN BY GUNS, CRESSY SOON FLOATED UPSIDE-DOWN LIKE HER SISTERS. OUT OF COMBINED CREWS OF 2,296, 1,459 MEN PERISHED.

WEDDIGEN AND HIS BOAT RECEIVED THE IRON CROSS FOR BRAVERY.

HE HAD REVEALED JUST HOW DEADLY U-BOATS COULD BE TO THE ALLIED NAVY.

THE END

UNDER SAVAGE FIRE

AT 15:48 HRS, MAY 31, 1916, THE GERMAN BATTLECRUISER, LUTZOW, LET LOOSE A DEAFENING BROADSIDE INTO THE WEST.

BOOMBAH!

VICE ADMIRAL HIPPER WATCHED THE VOLLEYS GO. HE WAS FOLLOWING ADMIRAL SCHEER'S MASTER PLAN, TO LURE TWO SQUADRONS OF BRITISH BATTLECRUISERS ...

...INTO AN **AMBUSH** BY SCHEER'S DREADNOUGHTS.

MAINTAIN HEADING SOUTH, SOUTHWEST.

LET'S LEAD THEM **ON**.

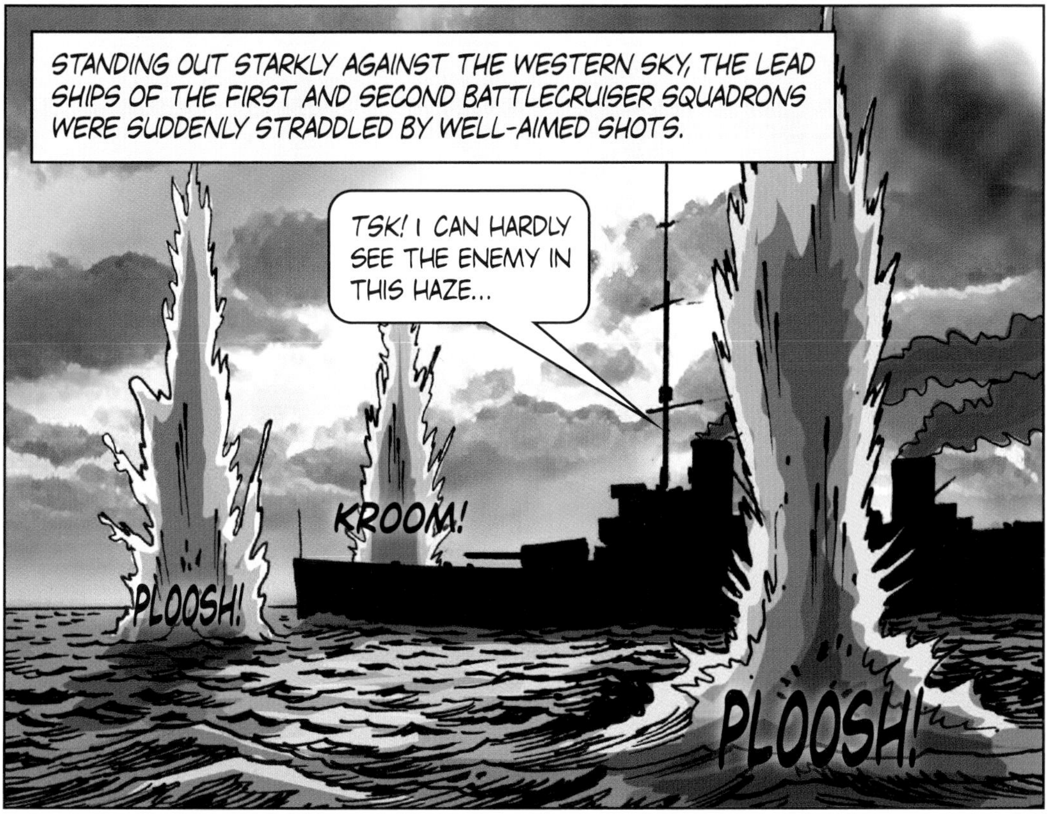
STANDING OUT STARKLY AGAINST THE WESTERN SKY, THE LEAD SHIPS OF THE FIRST AND SECOND BATTLECRUISER SQUADRONS WERE SUDDENLY STRADDLED BY WELL-AIMED SHOTS.
TSK! I CAN HARDLY SEE THE ENEMY IN THIS HAZE...
KROOM!
PLOOSH!
PLOOSH!

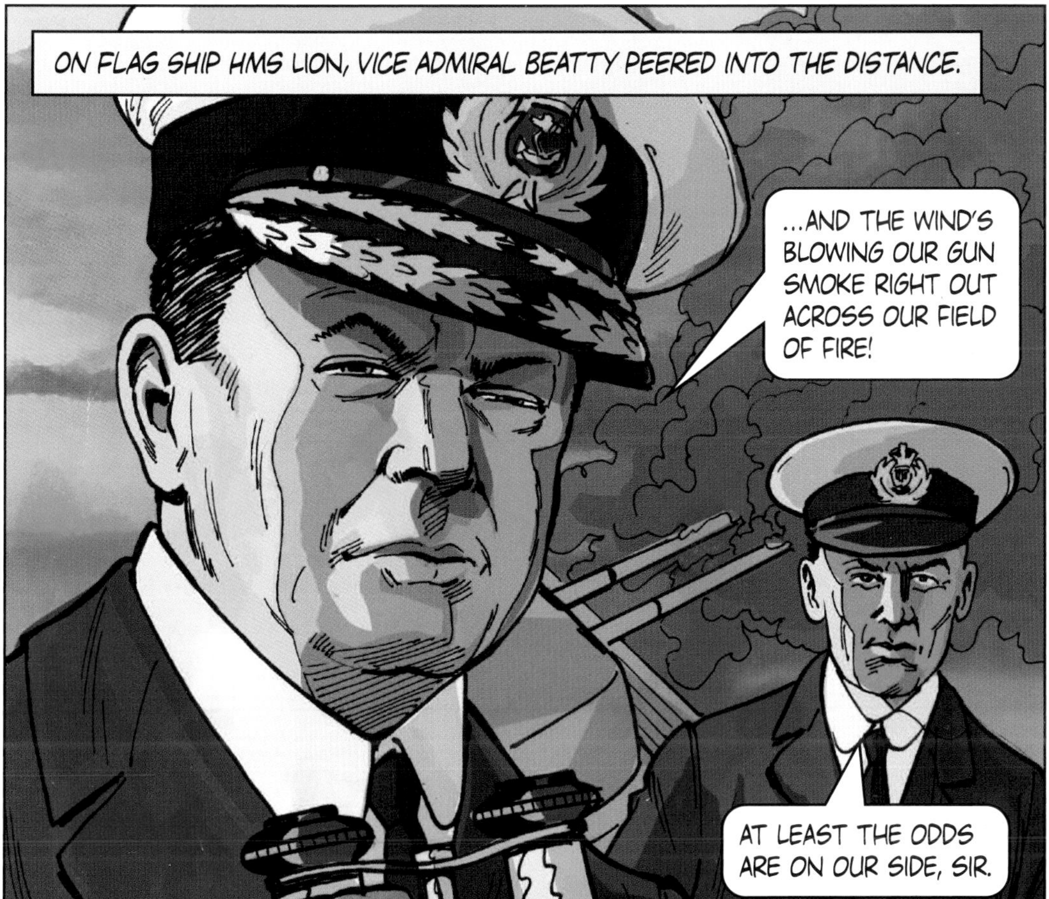
ON FLAG SHIP HMS LION, VICE ADMIRAL BEATTY PEERED INTO THE DISTANCE.
...AND THE WIND'S BLOWING OUR GUN SMOKE RIGHT OUT ACROSS OUR FIELD OF FIRE!
AT LEAST THE ODDS ARE ON OUR SIDE, SIR.

IT WAS SIX VERSUS FIVE AS THE REAR BRITISH SHIPS CAME INTO LINE AND ALL ELEVEN SHIPS BEGAN GIVING AND RECEIVING FIRE.

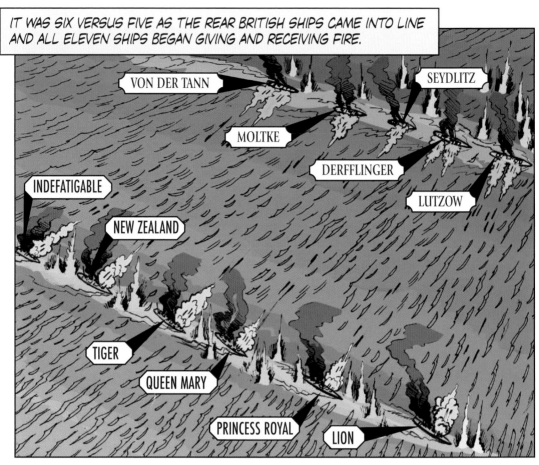

VON DER TANN

SEYDLITZ

MOLTKE

DERFFLINGER

LUTZOW

INDEFATIGABLE

NEW ZEALAND

TIGER

QUEEN MARY

PRINCESS ROYAL

LION

ALL EXCEPT THE DERFFLINGER.

SEE HOW THE BRITISH ARE OVERSHOOTING ALL OUR SHIPS!

SPLOOSH

SPLOOSH

SPLOOSH

JA! AND THEY ARE NOT EVEN TARGETING US!

KROOM

THE DERFFLINGER FIRED WITH ABANDON.

LION'S REAR CENTER TURRET (Q TURRET) EXPLODED IN FLAMES AS A MIRACULOUSLY-AIMED SHOT PENETRATED ITS TOP ARMOR.

FIZZZOOM!

CRACKLE!

INSIDE, MAJOR FRANCIS HARVEY, THE TURRET COMMANDER, STAGGERED TOWARD A VOICE PIPE.

IF THESE FIRES REACH THE CORDITE IN THE MAGAZINE BELOW, WE'RE ALL DONE FOR.

GNNNNGH!

THIS IS HARVEY. LOCK THE MAGAZINE ROOM AND FLOOD IT. *THAT'S AN ORDER!*

AYE, AYE, SIR!

GET TO IT!

MOMENTS LATER, HARVEY DIED.

ON LION'S BRIDGE...

FOOSH!

FOOSH!

Q TURRET IS GONE, SIR. ALL THE CREW ARE KILLED, AND WE HAVE FLOODED THE MAGAZINE.

WE'RE GETTING OUT OF RANGE. ALTER COURSE FOUR POINTS TO PORT.

THE REARMOST GERMAN SHIP, VON DER TANN, WAS ENGAGED IN A DUEL WITH HMS INDEFATIGABLE.

KRAKOOM!

SUDDENLY, INDEFATIGABLE WAS HIT BY THREE SHELLS AROUND THE REAR TURRET.

BOOM!

BOOM!

BOOM!

BADOOSH!

SEEMING TO LOSE POWER, SHE FELL OUT OF LINE, SINKING AT THE STERN.

RUMBLE

SHE WAS STRUCK BY MORE SHOTS, AND SUDDENLY EXPLODED.

KRAKOW!

ALL BUT THREE OF HER 1,017 CREW WERE KILLED INSTANTLY.

ONBOARD THE LUTZOW...

ADMIRAL, THE LEADING BRITISH SHIPS ARE HIDDEN BY SMOKE.

GET THE NEXT ONE VISIBLE.

THAT WAS THE QUEEN MARY.

INSIDE THE QUEEN MARY'S AFT BIG GUN TURRET, GUNNER'S MATE, E. FRANCIS, HAD BEEN HELPING TO TARGET THE SEYDLITZ.

TRANSMITTING STATION SAYS THE THIRD GERMAN HAS DROPPED OUT OF LINE!

HOORAH!

FIRST BLOOD TO THE MARY!

TAKE A LOOK FOR US!

FRANCIS CRANED UP TO HIS PERISCOPE.

YES, THERE'S DEFINITELY A GAP OPENED UP.

KROOM

KROOM

KROOM

KROOM

I THINK SHE'S GONE DOWN.

TONGUES OF FLAME ERUPTED FROM THE GUNS OF DERFFLINGER AND LUTZOW.

HMS QUEEN MARY WAS ROCKED BY HITS.

FIZZLE

CRACK!

BABOOM!

FRANCIS CHECKED THE PRESSURE GAUGE.

HYDRAULICS GONE. THE *TURRET'S* INOPERABLE!

THEN...

BOOM!

BOOM!

BOOM!

FRANCIS, STUNNED, DANGLED BY A SAFETY ROPE.

GASP!

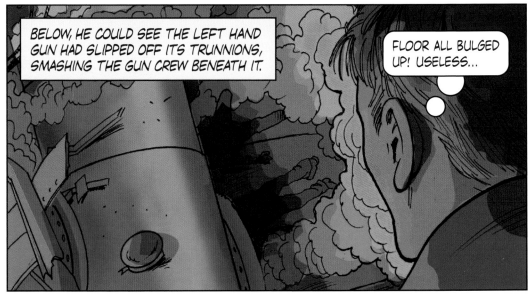

BELOW, HE COULD SEE THE LEFT HAND GUN HAD SLIPPED OFF ITS TRUNNIONS, SMASHING THE GUN CREW BENEATH IT.

FLOOR ALL BULGED UP! USELESS...

HE CLIMBED UP TO SEE IF THE SMALLER GUNS BEHIND COULD BE MANNED INSTEAD.

SITTING DUCKS IF WE'RE OUT OF ACTION.

THEY WERE SMASHED TO PIECES.

...AND WE'RE TILTING HEAVILY TO PORT.

THE ORDER WAS GIVEN TO CLEAR THE TURRET.

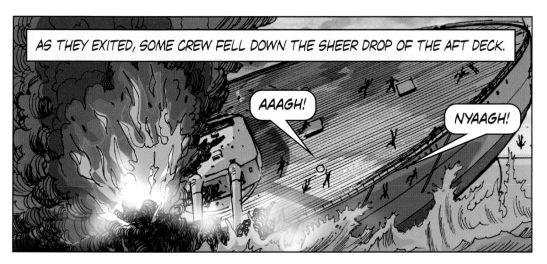

AS THEY EXITED, SOME CREW FELL DOWN THE SHEER DROP OF THE AFT DECK.

AAAGH!

NYAAGH!

SAILORS HELPED FRANCIS TO REACH THE STARBOARD SIDE.

COME ON! WE'VE GOT YOU.

MEN CLUNG TO THE HULL AS THE SHIP SLOWLY ROLLED.

WHO'S COMING FOR A SWIM THEN?

SHE'LL FLOAT FOR AGES YET!

SOMETHING IN HIS GUT URGED FRANCIS TO KEEP GOING.

ONBOARD LION, A HUGE PLUME OF FIRE ERUPTED FROM Q TURRET AS A FIRE IGNITED LOOSE SHELLS.

ROAAAR!

BUT THE FLOODED MAGAZINE KEPT THE WHOLE SHIP FROM EXPLODING.

A DEAFENING ROAR AND A MUSHROOM CLOUD OF SMOKE ROSE BEHIND FRANCIS AS HE SWAM AWAY FROM THE QUEEN MARY. TWO MORE GERMAN SHOTS HAD IGNITED HER AFT MAGAZINES, BLOWING HER TO PIECES.

KRACKOOM!

OUT OF A CREW OF 1,275, ONLY FRANCIS AND EIGHT OTHERS REMAINED ALIVE.

IT WAS NOW FOUR AGAINST FIVE.

CHATFIELD, THERE SEEMS TO BE SOMETHING WRONG WITH OUR SHIPS TODAY.

ALTER COURSE TWO POINTS TO STARBOARD.

AHEAD OF THE BATTLECRUISERS, LIGHT CRUISER SOUTHAMPTON HAD SPOTTED FUNNEL SMOKE.

BEARING NORTH, NORTHWEST. I COUNT AT LEAST A **DOZEN** SEPARATE SMOKE TRAILS.

IT'S SCHEER'S BATTLESHIPS— THE GERMAN HIGH SEAS FLEET!

SOON, BEATTY SAW THEM TOO.

IT'S A TRAP ALRIGHT.

SIGNAL THE SQUADRON. SIXTEEN POINT TURN TO STARBOARD IN SUCCESSION.

GERMAN FIRE HAD BECOME INACCURATE. THE SETTING SUN WAS BLINDING THE GUNNERS.

UNDER FIRE FROM HIPPER, THE FOUR BRITISH BATTLECRUISERS TURNED TO THE NORTH.

BEATTY'S PLAN WAS TO DRAW THE GERMAN BATTLECRUISERS AND BATTLESHIPS AFTER HIM.

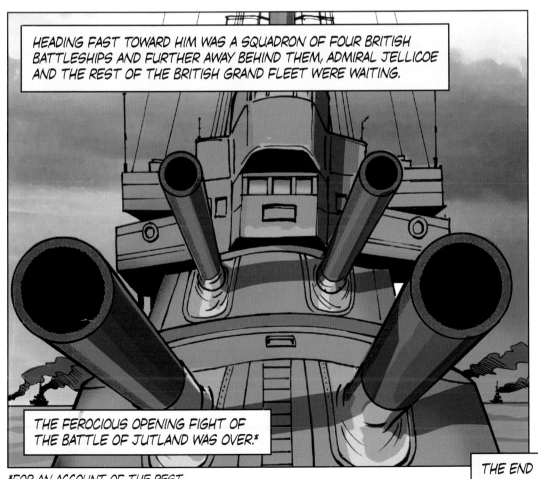

HEADING FAST TOWARD HIM WAS A SQUADRON OF FOUR BRITISH BATTLESHIPS AND FURTHER AWAY BEHIND THEM, ADMIRAL JELLICOE AND THE REST OF THE BRITISH GRAND FLEET WERE WAITING.

THE FEROCIOUS OPENING FIGHT OF THE BATTLE OF JUTLAND WAS OVER.*

THE END

*FOR AN ACCOUNT OF THE REST OF THE BATTLE, SEE PAGE 6

THE ZEEBRUGGE RAID

APRIL 23, 1918, ON THE BELGIAN COAST. WITH SMOKE SETTLING FAST, MOTOR BOATS SURGED AHEAD OF THE BRITISH NAVAL FLEET. ITS MISSION WAS TO BLOCK THE CANAL AT ZEEBRUGGE THAT ALLOWED GERMAN U-BOATS INTO THE NORTH SEA.

THE SMOKE SCREEN WAS LAID ACROSS HARBOR **MOLE***. BATTLESHIP **HMS** VINDICTIVE WAS TO ENTER AND TAKE OUT THE SHORE ARTILLERY WITH HER BIG GUNS.

*A MASSIVE WALL BUILT IN THE SEA
TO ENCLOSE OR PROTECT A HARBOR

ON THE BRIDGE OF VINDICTIVE.

THE SMOKE! IT'S BEING BLOWN CLEAR AWAY!

THIS IS WHERE THE FUN STARTS!

THEY'RE OPENING UP ON US WITH EVERYTHING THEY'VE GOT!

EXPOSED TO DEADLY FIRE, CAPTAIN CARPENTER GUIDED THE VINDICTIVE TO THE OUTSIDE OF THE MOLE.

OUR BIG GUNS WILL BE OUT OF IT, BUT AT LEAST THE HULL WILL BE SPARED.

FOOSH

AS SHE MANEUVERED INTO POSITION, VINDICTIVE RELEASED THE TWO CIVILIAN FERRIES SHE HAD BEEN TOWING. THEIR MISSION WAS TO LAND AN ASSAULT GROUP OF MARINES TO TAKE THE MOLE.

ON VINDICTIVE AND THE FERRY, IRIS, BOARDING PLANKS WERE LOWERED.

BUT THE TIDE WAS PUSHING THEM AWAY.

CLATTER!

THE CAPTAIN OF THE FERRY, DAFFODIL, ACTED QUICKLY.

BLAAR!

NOW THE MARINES ON DAFFODIL WERE STUCK, SOME CLIMBED OVER VINDICTIVE TO GET ASHORE.

THE REST WERE OUT OF THE GAME.

CREW ON IRIS TOSSED GRAPPLING HOOKS.

SIGNAL DAFFODIL TO KEEP PUSHING!

BUT THE MEN WHO TRIED TO FIX THE LINES WERE SHOT DOWN.

AAAGH!

MEANWHILE, OUTSIDE THE HARBOR, AN OLD SUBMARINE, WHOSE NOSE WAS PACKED WITH EXPLOSIVE, WAS BEING STEERED IN BY LIEUTENANT SANDFORD.

AS IT APPROACHED THE BRIDGE LINKING THE MOLE TO THE MAINLAND, THE ASTONISHED GERMANS EVEN STOPPED FIRING.

SANDFORD JAMMED THE SUB'S NOSE TIGHT UNDER THE BRIDGE...

THUMP!

...SET A FUSE, AND LEAPT OFF INTO A MOTOR BOAT.

THE BRIDGE AND EVERYONE ON IT WERE BLASTED HIGH INTO THE AIR.

KROOM

ROYAL MARINES SURGED UP AND ACROSS THE MOLE.

HAVE THEM!

CRACK!

DRRRRRRRRRRR

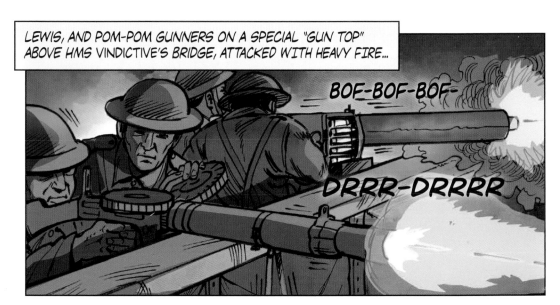

LEWIS, AND POM-POM GUNNERS ON A SPECIAL "GUN TOP" ABOVE HMS VINDICTIVE'S BRIDGE, ATTACKED WITH HEAVY FIRE...

BOF-BOF-BOF-

DRRR-DRRRR

...ATTRACTING THE ATTENTION OF THE GERMAN SHORE BATTERIES.

KROOM!

A SHELL DEMOLISHED THE "TOP."

BOUSH!

A SINGLE MARINE SURVIVED TO KEEP FIRING.

DRAAAAAGH!

IN THE HARBOR, THREE CONCRETE-FILLED "BLOCK SHIPS" WERE HEADING FULL-SPEED TOWARD THE CANAL ENTRANCE.

FOUSH!

THE LEAD SHIP THETIS CAME TO A SHUDDERING HALT.

IT'S NO GOOD—HER PROPELLERS ARE TANGLED IN NETS!

BANG!

AT LEAST WE'VE CLEARED THEM FOR THE OTHERS!

THE OTHER BLOCK SHIPS WERE HIT AND THEIR HULLS BLOWN.

GO! GO!

KROOM

KROOM!

BOOM!

THEY'VE DONE IT! THE CREWS ARE OFF IN MOTOR BOATS.

SOUND THE EVACUATION SIREN.

PEEOW!

I CAN'T, SIR. IT'S OUT OF ACTION.

SIGNAL DAFFODIL TO USE THEIRS.

THE FERRY'S WHISTLE WAS JUST BARELY AUDIBLE.

PWEEEEEEE

THE SURVIVORS FROM THE RAIDING PARTY CARRIED ABOARD AS MANY WOUNDED AND DEAD AS THEY COULD.

DRRRRR

ALL THE MEN ARE ABOARD, SIR!

TIME TO CAST OFF.

NOW WE'LL BE IN FOR IT.

IN THE VINDICTIVE'S BOILER ROOM...

THE OLD GIRL'S RATED AT EIGHTEEN KNOTS, BUT THE CAPTAIN WANTS TWENTY-ONE OUT OF HER!

GO TO IT!

WITH FLAMES BELCHING FROM THE HOLES IN HER FUNNELS, VINDICTIVE LED THE CHARGE AWAY FROM THE HARBOR. SMOKE BOATS CLOSED IN BEHIND THEM BUT COULDN'T SAVE THE IRIS, PACKED WITH MARINES WHO HADN'T MANAGED TO GET ON THE MOLE, FROM A SHELL THAT HIT AMIDSHIPS...

...KILLING 75 OF THEM, WHO THOUGHT THEY WERE SAFELY ON THEIR WAY HOME.

THERE WERE 583 CASUALTIES, INCLUDING 161 DEATHS. THE NEXT DAY, THIRTEEN BRITISH PRISONERS WERE MARCHED INTO THE PORT, PAST THE SUNKEN SHIPS THAT NOW BLOCKED THE BRUGES CANAL.

GOOD LUCK SHIFTING THAT LOT.

AT LAST THE ROYAL NAVY CAN HOLD HER HEAD HIGH AGAIN.

THE END

SCUTTLED!

During the Battle of Jutland, the Germans had the technological edge, with stronger ships and more powerful shells. But they remained hopelessly outnumbered. It was a victory of pride only.

The Germans declared a sinking zone around Great Britain and in the Mediterranean in 1917.

FLEET BOTTLED UP

German ship losses were made good within two months, but Britain still ruled the North Sea and the English Channel. After an aborted surface raid in September 1916, the Germans fell back on unrestricted submarine warfare to starve Britain of food and war materials. From February 1917, *any* ship, not just armed merchant vessels and warships, sailing in the war zone, would be attacked without warning by submerged U-boats. Germany was determined to win the war "by any means possible."

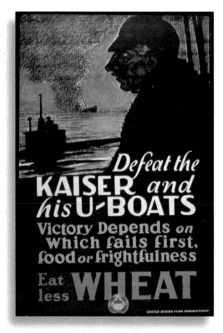

US propaganda seeks support against the U-boat campaign.

BLOCKADE BATTLES

By April 1917, more than a quarter of all Britain-bound ships were being sunk by U-boats. There was only six weeks worth of wheat left in the whole country. The loss of American ships and sailors finally pushed the United States to declare war on Germany on April 6, 1917.

Belatedly, a convoy system was introduced. The destroyers that escorted the convoys found more chances to attack U-boats that surfaced. Many more mines were laid, including an effective barrier across the English Channel. U-boat losses increased, while war-exhausted Germany struggled to replace them.

FINAL ACTS

The Imperial High Seas Fleet had one last role to play in the war. As armistice negotiations began, Scheer and Hipper planned a so-called "death ride"of all their ships to destroy as much of the British navy as possible.

Fortunately, their sailors disagreed and began a revolt on October 29, 1918, that spread and soon toppled the Kaiser himself. The victorious Allies ordered the High Seas Fleet to be interned at Scapa Flow in Orkney, Scotland, while peace negotiations determined how Germany's navy might be divided up amongst the victors if Germany agreed to the terms.

On the day of the deadline, June 21, 1919, Admiral Ludwig von Reuter, commander at Scapa, gave the order to scuttle, or sink, his ships. The British were outraged, the French and Italians disappointed, the Germans…unrepentant.

The pride of the German fleet was SMS **Bayern**, *their first ship to carry 15-inch (318 mm) main guns. They were never fired in anger.*

SMS **Bayern** *lies sinking in Scapa Flow, along with 51 others in the Imperial German Navy's last act of aggression.*

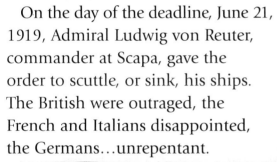

The U-boat force surrendered together at Harwich in Britain, in November, 1918. They were all destroyed.

GLOSSARY

aggressive Forceful, militant, menacing

amidships In or toward the middle part of a ship

armistice An agreement between opposing armies to stop fighting in order to discuss peace terms

arms race A competition between countries to have the best and largest amount of military arms

batteries Groups of military artillery such as heavy guns

bombardment An attack with concentrated artillery fire or bombs

bow The front of a ship

broadside The entire side of a ship

capsize To overturn a ship or boat

casualties Those in hostile engagements that die, are captured, or go missing

cautious To be careful, watchful or guarded

flotilla A group of small naval vessels

hull The frame of the bottom of a ship

Imperial naval code A set of laws or rules that the navy must follow

infamy An evil or criminal act that is publicly known

interception To take or seize something intended for someone else

isolated To be separated and alone

HMS Invincible *blows up during the fleet battle at Jutland, on May 31, 1916.*

lure To attract or draw in; baiting

magazine A building used for storing weapons and explosives

miraculous An unexpected event that is amazing or wonderful

momentous Something that is of great importance or consequence

penetrated To have pierced, passed into, or passed through

periscope A device that uses mirrors to provide a view of an object that is above or below direct sight

port Left side of a ship

pummeling Beating or thrashing

ramming To strike violently with great force

reluctant Unwilling to do something

rendezvous An agreement between two or more people to meet at a certain place and time

scuttle To sink or try to sink a ship by making holes through the bottom of the hull

squadron A unit in the air force consisting of two or more flights

starboard The right side of a ship

torpedo Submarine explosive devices used to destroy hostile ships

turret A dome-like structure, capable of rotation, that houses guns and gunners

unleash To free from restraint

winch The handle of a machine that revolves

SMS Seydlitz after limping back to port with heavy damage in June 1916.

INDEX